Canadian Curriculum ScienceSmart

Grade 4

ISBN: 978-1-927042-86-1

Printed in China

Contents

ISBN: 978-1-927042-86-1

ISBN: 978-1-927042-86-1

ISBN: 978-1-927042-86-1

Habitats and Communities (1)

1

In this unit, students will:

- identify the needs of some animals.
- identify the habitats of different animals.
- identify the habitats of different plants.

ISBN: 978-1-927042-86-1

1

A. Fill in the chart with the habitat bits. Answer the questions.

Habitat Bits

- water plants and tiny water animals
- acorns, seeds, and berries
- open ocean/shallow water for feeding
- natural hole in a tree
- seals and sea lions
- dam and lodge
- cambium
- marsh
- stream

Science Corner

Every living thing has needs: a place to live and food to eat. An organism's habitat is that place.

Cambium is a soft part of the inside of a tree where new wood growth happens.

1.	Food	Habitat	Shelter
Wood Duck			
Beaver			
White Shark			

2. What is the habitat of whales? ____________

3. What is your habitat? ____________

ISBN: 978-1-927042-86-1

B. **List the names of animals in the correct columns. Then write one more animal for each column.**

duck fish caterpillar mole worm

robin tadpole beetle owl

groundhog mosquito ant goose mite

millipede turtle monkey koala

Animal Habitats and Their Animals

1 Pond	2 Soil	3 Tree

ISBN: 978-1-927042-86-1

C. **Write the name of the animal that belongs in each verse.**

1. I am a ______________

   From the sky I can see
   The fish to bring back
   To my nest in a tree.

2. I am a ______________

   I need to keep moist
   Under rocks, under logs
   Underneath is my choice.

3. I am a ______________

   I live underground
   In forests and meadows
   Where my supper is found.

4. I am a ______________

   Of trees I am fond
   They're my shelter, my food
   My dam for my pond.

Science Corner

A fallen tree becomes a habitat for animals from insects to deer, providing food and shelter.

ISBN: 978-1-927042-86-1

D. Read the plant descriptions and match the plants with where they are found.

A

B

C

1. • small plants growing close to the ground
   • shallow roots
   • buds with a fuzzy covering
   • dark purple leaves to absorb heat

2. • flexible stems
   • small roots used to anchor the plant
   • many small leaves
   • many air-filled spaces

3. • a waxy skin to hold water
   • shallow and wide roots
   • large spines to protect itself from animals

ISBN: 978-1-927042-86-1

1

Try this!

Snails' Habitats

Materials:

- a big container
- food wrap
- some paper towels
- water

Steps:

1. Put a wet paper towel in one half of the container and a dry one in the other half.
2. Put the snails in the container.
3. Cover the container with the food wrap.
4. Observe the snails for a few minutes.

Where do the snails choose to stay on? Do you know why?

____

____

____

Checklist

Are you able to...

- ☐ identify the needs of some animals?
- ☐ identify the habitats of different animals?
- ☐ identify the habitats of different plants?

ISBN: 978-1-927042-86-1

Habitats and Communities (2)

2

In this unit, students will:

- understand the relationship between producers and consumers.
- identify producers and consumers.
- understand the definitions of carnivore, herbivore, and omnivore and classify animals into these three groups.
- describe ways in which human beings are dependent on plants and animals.

ISBN: 978-1-927042-86-1

2

A. Fill in the blanks and answer the questions with the given words.

community **consumers** **producers** **sun**

1. The light from the ________________ gives the world energy. Plants use sunlight to make food. We call them ________________ .

2. Animals cannot make their own food. They must eat other living things. They are called ________________ .

3. The name that we give to the group of plants and animals living in a habitat is ________________ .

4. What are consumers dependent on for survival?

____

5. What is the energy source for producers?

____

ISBN: 978-1-927042-86-1

B. List all the labelled producers and consumers in the correct columns.

Temperate Woodland

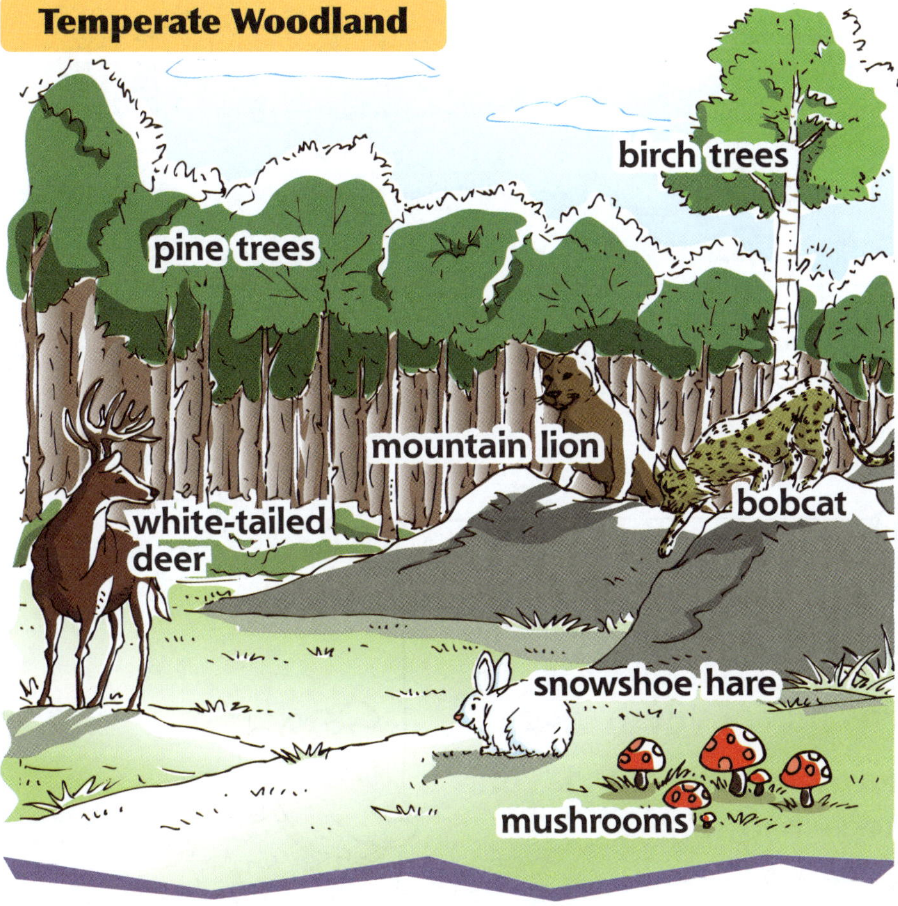

Tundra

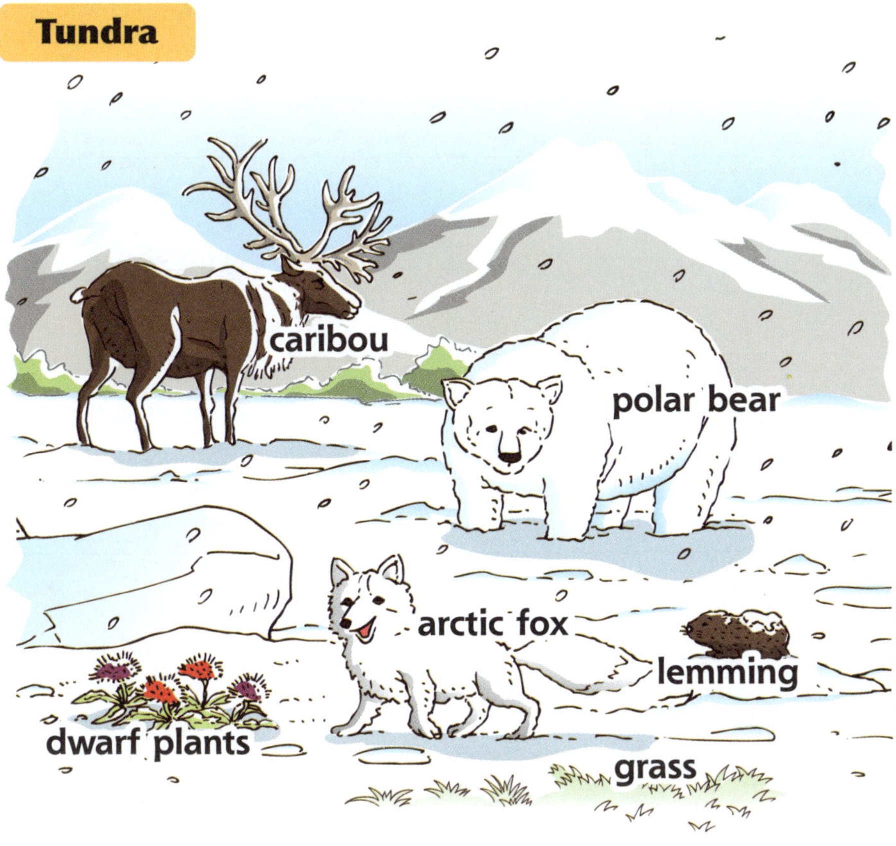

Producer

____

____

____

____

____

Consumer

____

____

____

____

____

____

____

____

2

C. Read what Howard says. Then write the definitions of the words and answer the question.

All consumers eat living things. There are three different types of consumers. Look at the roots of three of our English words that describe the types of consumers. Use the clues to help decide what each word means. Then classify the animals according to what they eat.

1. Definition

   • Carnivore: ______________________________

   e.g. ______________

   • Herbivore: ______________________________

   e.g. ______________

   • Omnivore: ______________________________

   e.g. ______________

2. What kind of "vore" are you? ______________

ISBN: 978-1-927042-86-1

D. Human beings depend on plants and animals for survival. Look at the pictures. Then tell what they are used for.

clothing food medicine shelter travel

1.

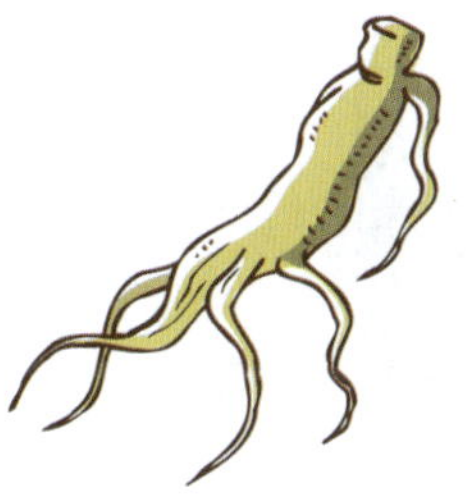

____

2.

____

3.

____

4.

____

5.

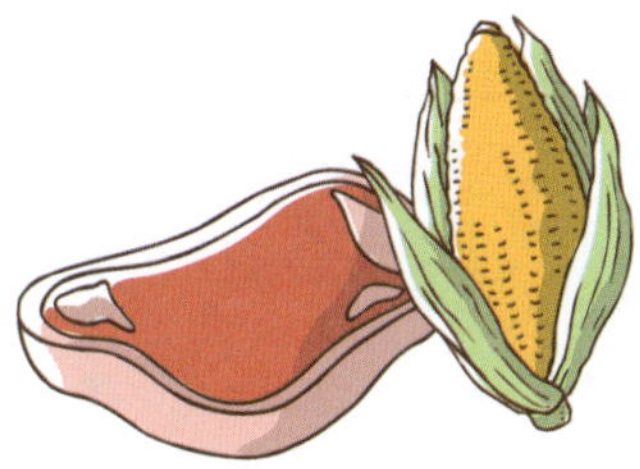

____

6.

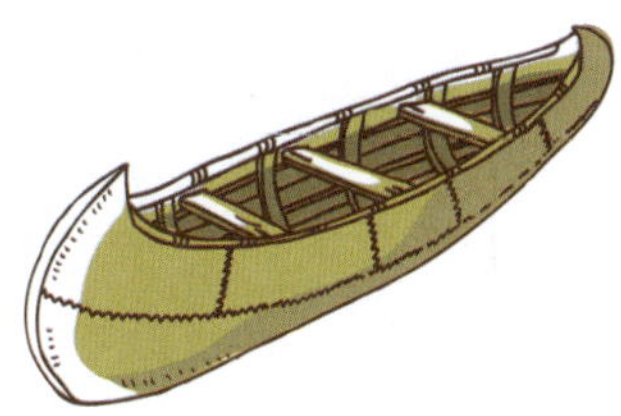

____

7.

A ________________

B ________________

ISBN: 978-1-927042-86-1

2

Try this!

We Are So Dependent!

Thing	From plant/animal	Used for

Checklist

Are you able to...

- [ ] explain the relationship between producers and consumers?
- [ ] identify producers and consumers?
- [ ] define carnivore, herbivore, and omnivore and classify animals into these three groups?
- [ ] describe ways in which human beings are dependent on plants and animals?

ISBN: 978-1-927042-86-1

Food Chains

3

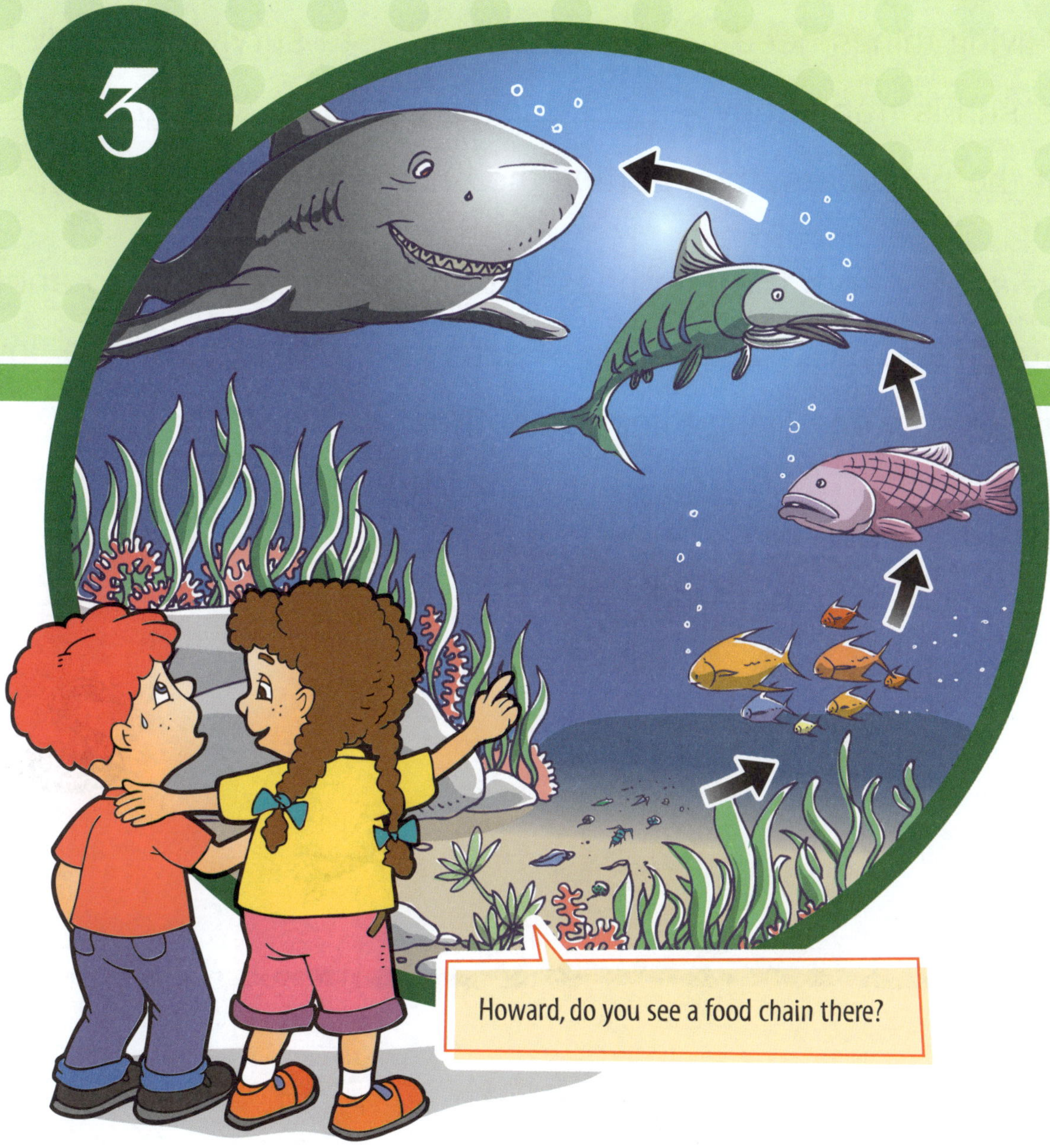

In this unit, students will:

- understand the meaning of a food chain as a system to show the flow of energy.
- construct food chains.
- understand the importance of maintaining a balanced food chain.

ISBN: 978-1-927042-86-1

3

A. **Fill in the blanks with the given words to complete the paragraphs. Then trace the correct arrows to complete the food chains.**

consumers	energy	food chains	producers

All living things need 1. ________________ to survive. Energy from the sun is trapped by 2. ________________ . 3. ________________ eat the producers, thus getting the energy in a different way.

The energy from the sun passes from one living thing to another through 4. ________________ . Each arrow there shows the flow of energy from one living thing to another.

5.

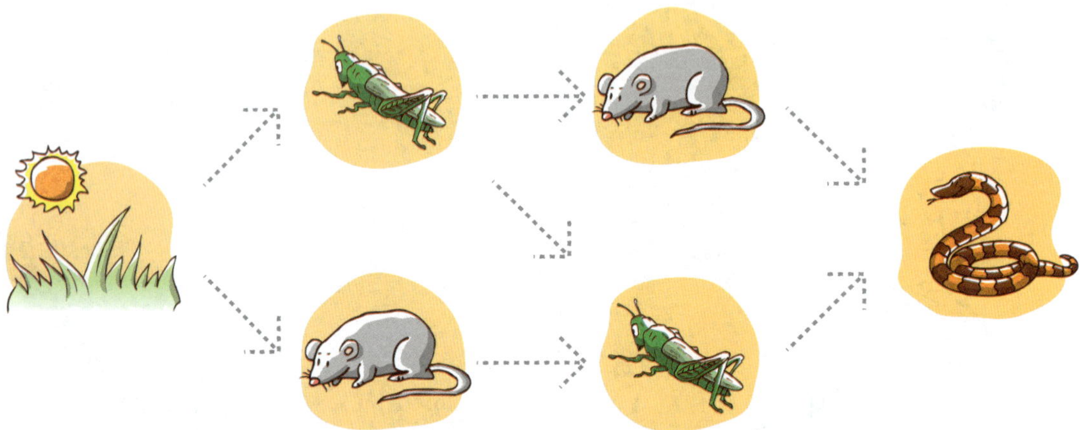

6.

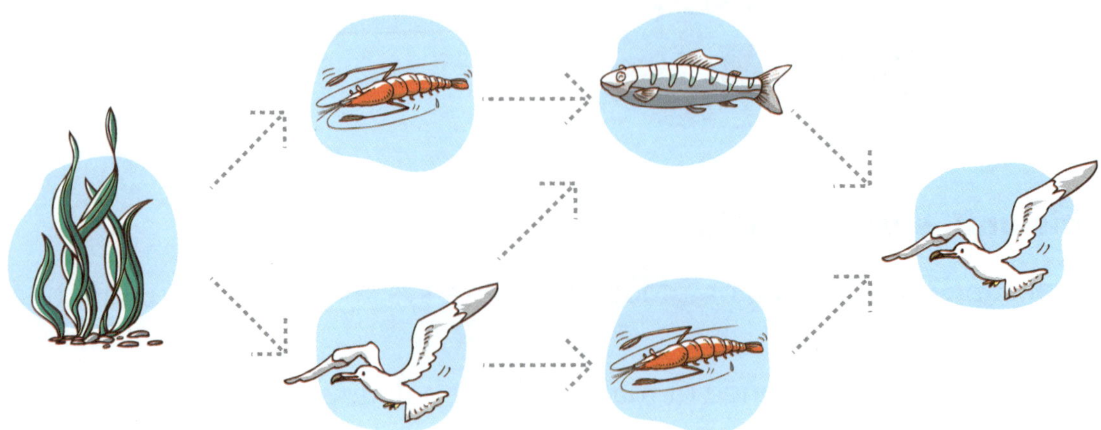

 ISBN: 978-1-927042-86-1

B. **For each group of living things, write each organism's name in the proper spot in the food chain.**

A
owl
plant
mouse

B
grass
red fox
rabbit
tiger

C
shark
plankton
shrimp
small fish
big fish

D
insect
sage brush
snake
lizard
hawk

Food Chain

A ______________ → ______________ → ______________

B ____

C ____

D ____

ISBN: 978-1-927042-86-1

3

C. Read what Justin says. Fill in the blanks with the given words. Then complete and label the organisms in the food chain.

break disappear healthy food chains

The energy from the sun passes from one living thing to another through 1. ____________ . 2. ____________ habitats have the living things in the food chains in balance. If habitats are changed too much, some of the living things in the food chains 3. ____________ . The chains 4. ____________ .

5. Complete the food chain with the organisms below and tell whether they are "producer", "herbivore", or "carnivore".

____________ → ____________ → ____________

 ISBN: 978-1-927042-86-1

D. Look at the food chain on the previous page again. Read what Andy says. Answer the questions.

Imagine that there is just enough grass to feed the zebras, and just enough zebras to keep the lions fed. The habitat is balanced. Now, look at each situation below and answer the questions.

Situation 1

What two things would happen if the herbivores were removed from this food chain?

a. ______________________________

b. ______________________________

Situation 2

What two things would happen if the producers were removed from this food chain?

a. ______________________________

b. ______________________________

Situation 3

What two things would happen if the carnivores were removed from this food chain?

a. ______________________________

b. ______________________________

Why is it important for us to protect other living things?

____

ISBN: 978-1-927042-86-1

3

Try this!

Food Chain Game

Write each organism's name on a card. Then put the cards face down to start this game.

Materials:

- 30 cards of size 3 cm by 4 cm each

grass	grasshopper	rabbit
hawk	lion	owl
snake	mouse	clover
frog	ant	wheat
spider	fly	shrimp
tree	caterpillar	seal
gull	salmon	polar bear
fox	snail	bear
blackberry	squirrel	penguin
monkey	chicken	worm

Make a chart to record your scores.

Round / Player	1st	2nd	3rd	4th

Game:

Each player takes turn to pick 5 cards. Make a food chain as long as possible. Give yourself 1 point for every organism in your chain. The person who gets the most points wins.

Checklist

Are you able to...

- ☐ explain why a food chain is a system to show the flow of energy?
- ☐ construct food chains?
- ☐ tell the importance of maintaining a balanced food chain?

ISBN: 978-1-927042-86-1

Adaptations of Living Things

In this unit, students will:

- identify the structural adaptations of birds.
- identify the structural adaptations of insects.
- understand the behavioural adaptations of different animals to their environments.

ISBN: 978-1-927042-86-1

4

A. Look at the beaks of different birds. Tell how the birds with their particular beaks adapt to the lives that they lead. Match the pictures with the correct descriptions.

1. ...tearing flesh is the main job here.
2. ...it uses its beak to crack the shells of seeds to reach the nutritious interior that makes up its diet.
3. ...just like a straw that you'd see in a milkshake, this one sips!
4. ...it uses its beak to strain small plants and animals from the water.
5. ...tapping tree trunks noisily to make your head ache.

 ISBN: 978-1-927042-86-1

B. Look at the facts about different birds. Match the pictures with the correct adaptations.

1. The power in these claws must be great to hold on to the supper.

   ______

2. They are designed for perching. These claws are sure to keep their owner secure on twigs.

   ______

3. You can really see how we have copied nature's design here. Scuba divers should thank the ducks!

   ______

4. Its long, strong toes with curved tails can grab bark tightly. That's why it is a good climber.

   ______

5. This funny bird can run, but not fly, fast with its three-toed feet.

   ______

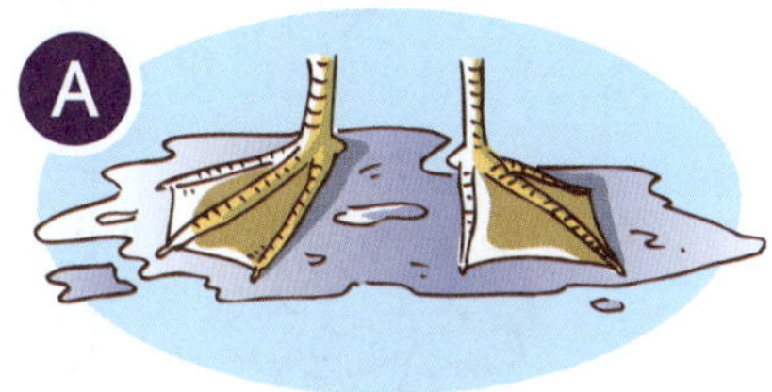

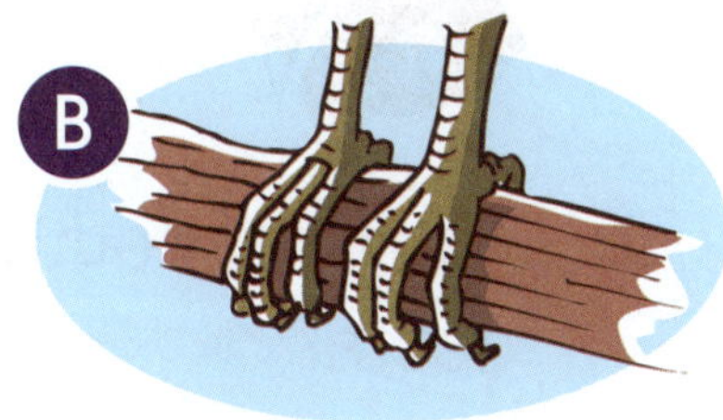

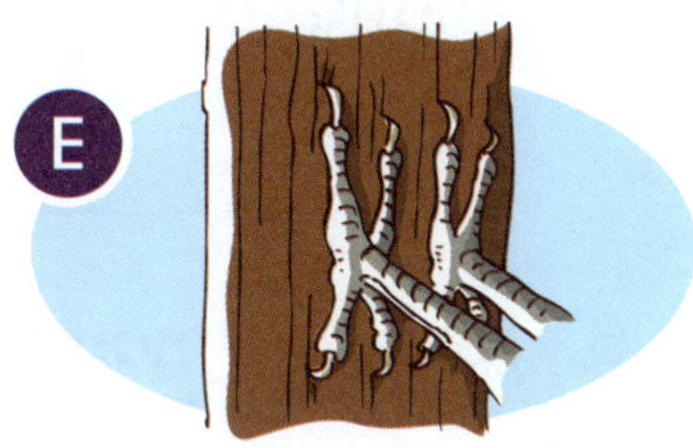

ISBN: 978-1-927042-86-1

4

C. Insects have different types of organs for obtaining and eating food. Read the clues and match them with the correct insects.

1. 

...coiled tube that is used to suck nectar out of a flower.

____

2. chewing mouth parts and tongue that act like a pump to gather nectar

____

3. piercing, sucking, or sponging mouth parts

____

4. mandibles to chew and to fight with

____

5. strong mouth parts to be able to chew through bark and phloem; mouth parts move in a cutting motion like scissors

____

6. piercing mouth parts – only the females suck blood

____

ISBN: 978-1-927042-86-1

D. Check the correct answers.

Science Corner

Some of the adaptations that animals have show up in the way they act or behave. These adaptations are called "behavioural adaptations". These adaptations do what all adaptations do – help living things survive in their habitats.

1. Animals such as lions hunt in groups because

   (A) **they like the company.**

   (B) **larger and faster animals can be caught.**

   (C) **they are afraid to act alone.**

2. The opossum has a way to avoid being eaten by predators that eat moving prey. It

   (A) **outruns its would-be eater.**

   (B) **plays dead.**

   (C) **begs for mercy.**

3. During the winter, to avoid cold temperatures and food shortages, brown bears

   (A) **migrate to Florida.**

   (B) **hibernate.**

   (C) **look for heated homes.**

4. Chimpanzees change twigs into tools so that they can

   (A) **better dig for termites that live under the ground.**

   (B) **be more like us.**

   (C) **get us to say, "Cool!"**

ISBN: 978-1-927042-86-1

4

Try this!

"Pipe Cleaner" Insects

Materials:

- 16 30-cm coloured pipe cleaners (2 red, 2 green, 2 yellow, 2 orange, 2 brown, 2 black, 2 white, and 2 purple)
- one paper bag for each player
- one long string (about 25 m long)

Steps:

1. Cut each pipe cleaner into 15 pieces that are about the same length. These will be insects.
2. Make a big circle with the string in your backyard. Then spread the cut pipe cleaners evenly in the enclosed area.
3. The players then go into the circle and pick as many "insects" as they can in one minute.

The "insects" in which colours are collected the least? Do you know why?

____

____

Checklist

Are you able to...

- ☐ identify the structural adaptations of birds?
- ☐ identify the structural adaptations of insects?
- ☐ describe the behavioural adaptations of different animals to their environments?

 ISBN: 978-1-927042-86-1

Light

5

In this unit, students will:

- understand the meaning of natural and artificial light.
- identify objects that emit light and those that reflect light.
- identify objects that give off both light and heat, and those that give off light but produce no heat.
- understand the meaning of spectrum.
- understand the behaviour of light reflection and refraction.

ISBN: 978-1-927042-86-1

5

A. Fill in the blanks with the given words.

artificial **natural**

We get light from many different sources. Light that occurs in nature is 1. ________________ light. Light that is created by people, and does not occur naturally, is 2. ________________ light.

B. Circle the light sources in the picture. Then list them in the correct columns.

Natural Light	Artificial Light

ISBN: 978-1-927042-86-1

C. **Fill in the blanks to complete what Michael says. Then identify each object as a light source or a reflector. Write "light source" or "reflector" in the box.**

emit **reflect**

Most things do not 1. ____________ their own light but we see them because light bounces off them. They 2. ____________ light. Some things reflect light better than others.

3.

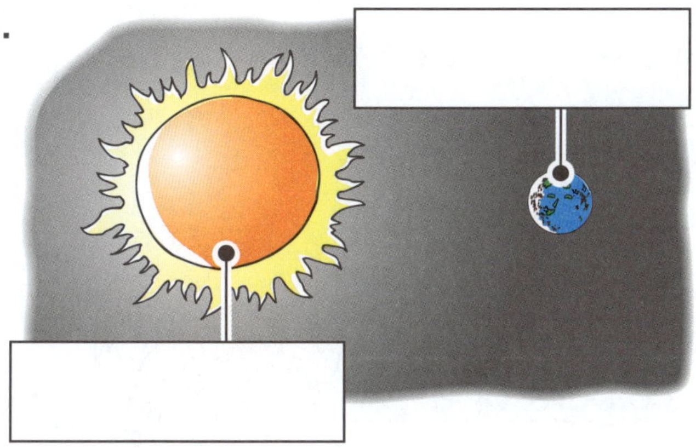

4.

5.

ISBN: 978-1-927042-86-1

5

D. Identify each picture as a natural light or an artificial light. Then tell whether it "gives off heat" or "produces no heat".

1.

2.

3.

_______________ _______________ _______________

_______________ _______________ _______________

E. Fill in the blanks with the given words to complete what Cathy says.

rainbow spectrum white

There are many colours in a ray of sunlight. Mixed together, we see them as 1. _______________ , but in that white light is all the colours of a 2. _______________ . A rainbow occurs when light rays pass through water droplets in the air. The light bends and splits into the individual colours it is made up of. This is called the 3. _______________ .

ISBN: 978-1-927042-86-1

F. Fill in the blanks with the given words. Then colour the correct examples.

reflection refraction

1. When a light ray hits an object and bounces off, it is a ______________ .

An example of reflection:

2. Light travels in a straight line, but when it passes through another medium such as water, it may bend and change direction. This is called ______________ .

An example of refraction:

G. Tell whether each situation is an example of reflection or refraction.

1. I see a fish in the water, but I know it is not exactly where I see it. ______________

2. The moon does not emit its own light but it shines brightly in the night sky. ______________

ISBN: 978-1-927042-86-1

5

Try this!

Light and Heat

Take a look around your house and find things that emit light. In the chart, record the name of each thing and where you find it. Note down its colour and whether or not it gives off heat.

Light			
Thing	Place	Colour	Heat

Checklist

Are you able to...

- [ ] tell the difference between natural and artificial light?
- [ ] identify objects that emit light and those that reflect light?
- [ ] identify objects that give off both light and heat, and those that give off light but not heat?
- [ ] explain what spectrum is?
- [ ] explain the behaviour of light reflection and refraction?

ISBN: 978-1-927042-86-1

A. Complete the crossword puzzle.

It is a ____________.

a habitat for ducks, frogs, and geese

We use some plants and animals for this.

animals that eat only plants

All living things need this to survive.

an example of ____________

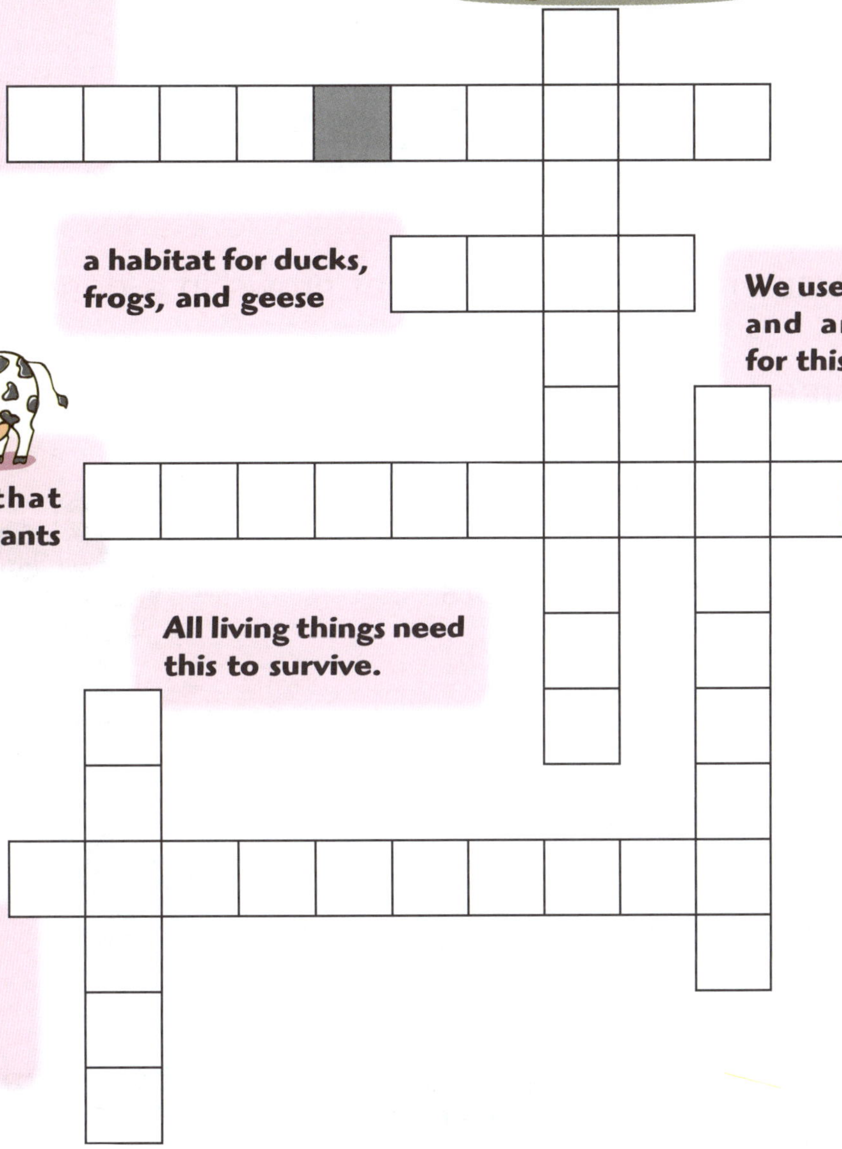

carnivores energy food chain herbivores

pond refraction medicine

ISBN: 978-1-927042-86-1

B. Check the correct answers.

1. Examples of artificial light:

(A) 

(B) 

(C) 

(D) 

(E) 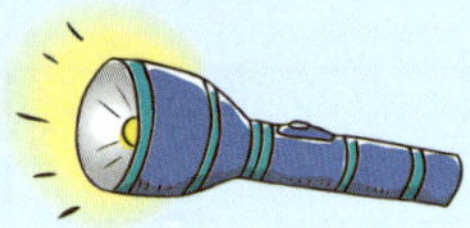

(F) 

2. The characteristics of a plant that grows in a desert:

(A) large spines to protect itself from animals

(B) a waxy skin to hold water

(C) shallow and wide roots

(D) flexible stems

3. The correct food chains:

(A) 

(B) 

(C) 

(D) 

ISBN: 978-1-927042-86-1

4. Birds with these feet 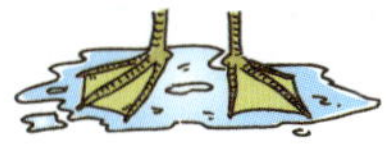 are especially adapted to live in

(A) forests.

(B) caves.

(C) ponds.

(D) trees.

5. Birds with this beak  are good at

(A) cracking shells.

(B) tearing flesh.

(C) tapping tree trunks.

(D) straining small animals.

6. Things that use sunlight  to make food:

(A) 

(B) 

(C) 

(D) 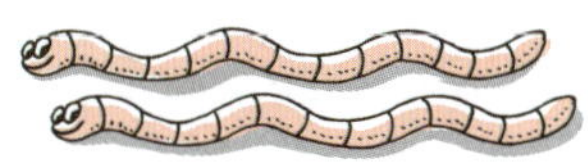

7. If the herbivores were removed from the food chain below, two things that would happen are:

(A) The amount of grass would decrease.

(B) The amount of grass would increase.

(C) The number of foxes would stay the same.

(D) The number of foxes would decrease.

ISBN: 978-1-927042-86-1

C. Help the children complete the sentences about light.

- water drops in the air bend sunlight
- is an example of a light source
- in straight lines from the light source
- refraction
- refracts, displaying the seven colours of the visible spectrum

1. Light travels ____ .

2. A pencil, when placed in a glass of water, appears to be broken because of ____ .

3. The sun ____ .

4. When white light passes through a prism, it ____________________ ____ .

5. A rainbow appears when ____________ ____________________ ____________________ .

 ISBN: 978-1-927042-86-1

Sound

6

In this unit, students will:

- record the sounds encountered in different places and describe the loudness.
- use standard units to measure the loudness of sounds.
- learn how sounds are produced by different musical instruments.
- identify the uses of sounds.

ISBN: 978-1-927042-86-1

6

A. Go somewhere to sit down and listen. As you hear a sound, make an entry in this chart. Fill in all the columns.

Suggested places:

- park
- canteen
- backyard
- library
- restaurant

Science Corner

Sound is energy. Whenever anything vibrates, it makes sounds. The larger the vibration, the louder the sound.

Sound Heard (Who/What is making it?)	Loudness (soft/loud)	Location of Sound (close/far away)

ISBN: 978-1-927042-86-1

B. **Match the readings with the correct pictures.**

100 dB 25 dB 10 dB

80 dB 180 dB 120 dB

Science Corner

Sound is measured in "decibels" (dB). Sounds above 130 dB are dangerous. Hearing may be damaged immediately.

1.

______

2.

______

3.

______

4.

______

5.

______

6.

______

ISBN: 978-1-927042-86-1

6

C. **Complete the descriptions. Then sort the musical instruments into the correct groups. Write the letters.**

having strings that vibrate   being struck
having air blown into it

A

B
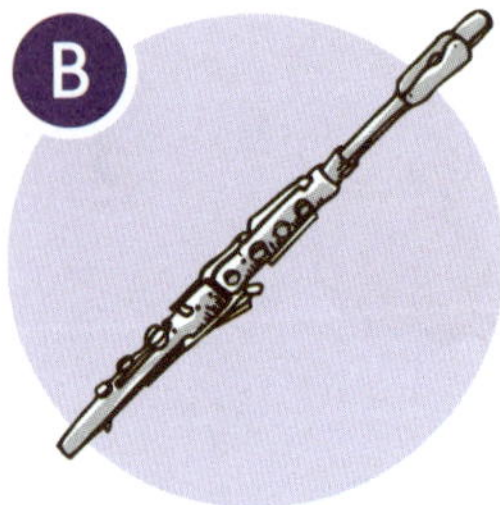

C

D

E
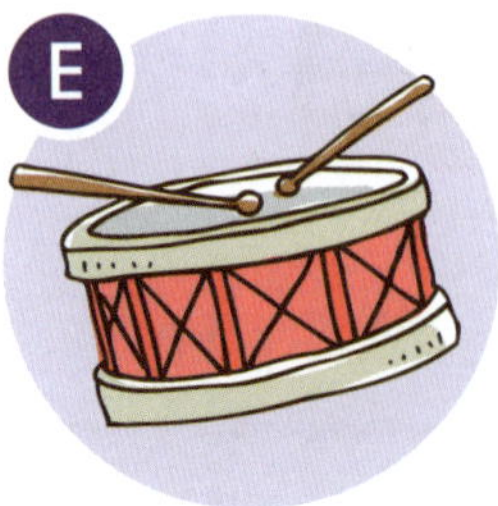

F

1. **Percussion Instrument:**
   makes sounds by ________
   ____
   Examples: ◯ ◯

2. **Wind Instrument:**
   makes sounds by ________
   ____
   Examples: ◯ ◯

3. **String Instrument:**
   makes sounds by ________
   ____
   Examples: ◯ ◯

ISBN: 978-1-927042-86-1

D. Identify the uses of sounds. Write the answers on the lines.

alarming sound   detecting sound   soothing sound

1.

____

2.

____

3.

____

4.

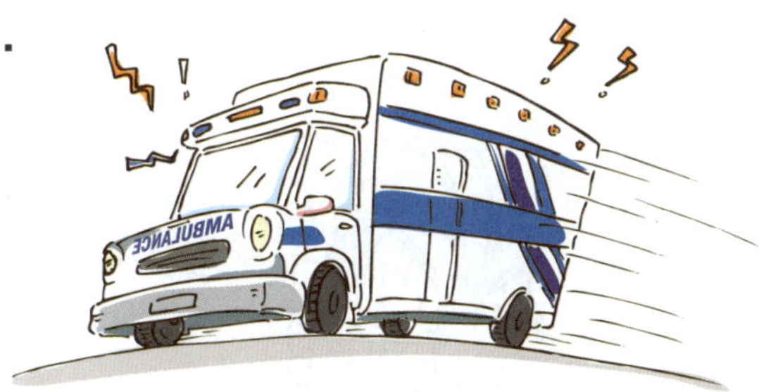

____

5.

____

6.

____

E. Give one example of each type of sound.

alarming sound: ______________________

detecting sound: ______________________

soothing sound: ______________________

ISBN: 978-1-927042-86-1

6

Try this!

My Musical Instrument

You can make your own musical instrument with just a clothes hanger, some strings, and some nuts, bolts, and other small metal objects. Wind can make music for you if you just let it! Hang the metal objects from the clothes hanger using the strings. Make sure the objects are allowed to hit each other when they move. Let the music begin!

The stronger the wind is, the louder the music!

Checklist

Are you able to...

- ☐ record the sounds encountered in different places and describe the loudness?
- ☐ use standard units to measure the loudness of sounds?
- ☐ explain how sounds are produced by different musical instruments?
- ☐ identify the uses of sounds?

ISBN: 978-1-927042-86-1

7 Gears

In this unit, students will:

- identify objects that have gears in their mechanisms.
- make gears to recognize the direction of movements of the gears.
- make gears to recognize the speeds of the gears.

ISBN: 978-1-927042-86-1

7

A. Look at each picture. Check the ones with gears and cross out those without gears.

1.

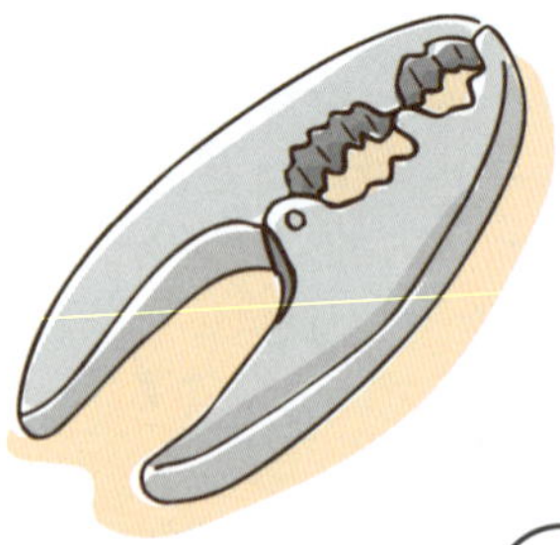

2.

Science Corner

Mechanisms are the working parts of machines. Gears are often found in machines.

3.

4.

5.

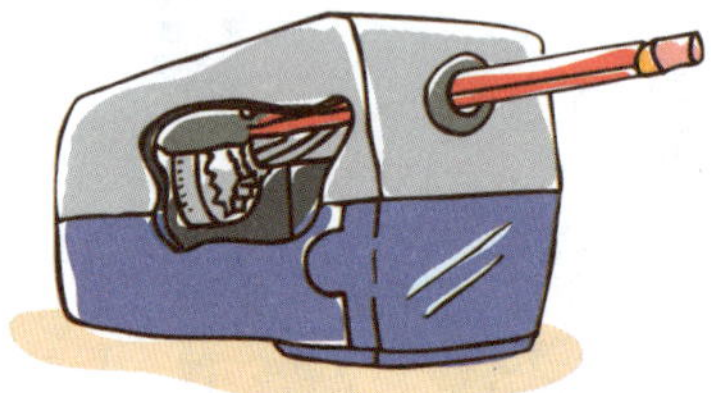

6.

7.

8.

ISBN: 978-1-927042-86-1

B. Follow the steps to make gears. Then answer the questions on the next page.

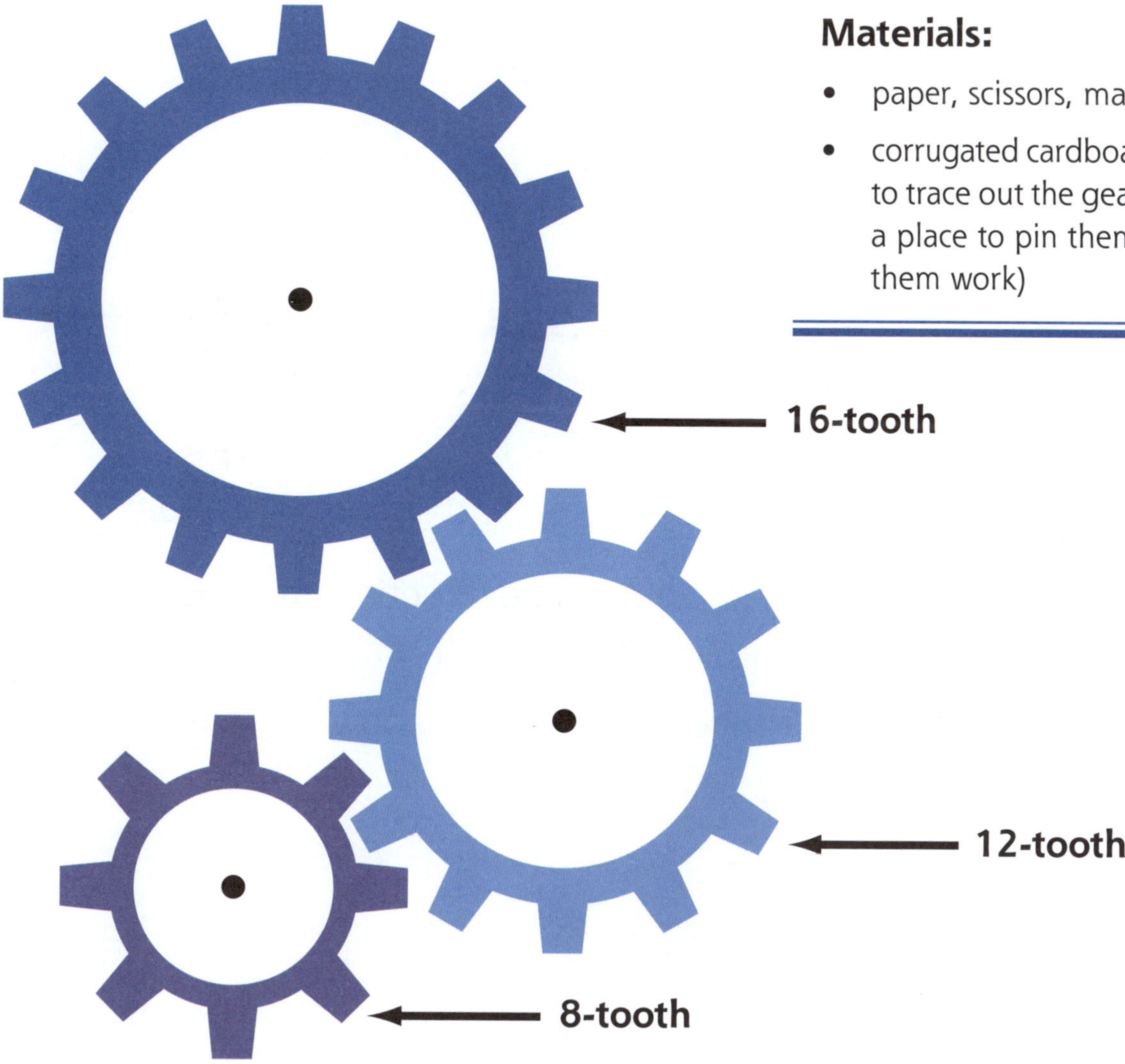

Materials:

- paper, scissors, marker, pins
- corrugated cardboard (enough to trace out the gears and have a place to pin them and make them work)

Steps:

1. Trace the gears onto a piece of paper and cut them out. Make one big (16-tooth), one medium (12-tooth), and two small (8-tooth) gears.
2. Use these as stencils to trace the gears on corrugated cardboard. Cut the cardboard gears out.
3. On each gear, mark one of the teeth with a marker. Mark the centre as well.
4. Use pins to pin the centre of the gears on a sheet of cardboard to set the gears up as shown on the next page.

ISBN: 978-1-927042-86-1

7

C. Set the gears up as shown. Then answer the questions.

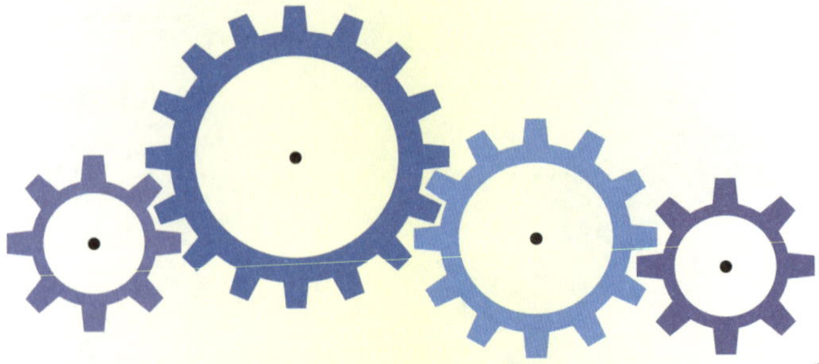

1. Turn one of the gears. What happens to the other gears?

____

2. If you turn the first one in a clockwise direction, in what directions do the second, the third, and the fourth ones turn?

   Draw arrows in the spaces provided to show the directions.

3. If there is one more gear set after the fourth gear, in what direction will the fifth gear turn?

   ____

4. Do you think gears can change the direction of rotation?

   ____

ISBN: 978-1-927042-86-1

D. Set the gears up as shown to explore what happens when gears of different sizes are used together. Then circle the correct answers.

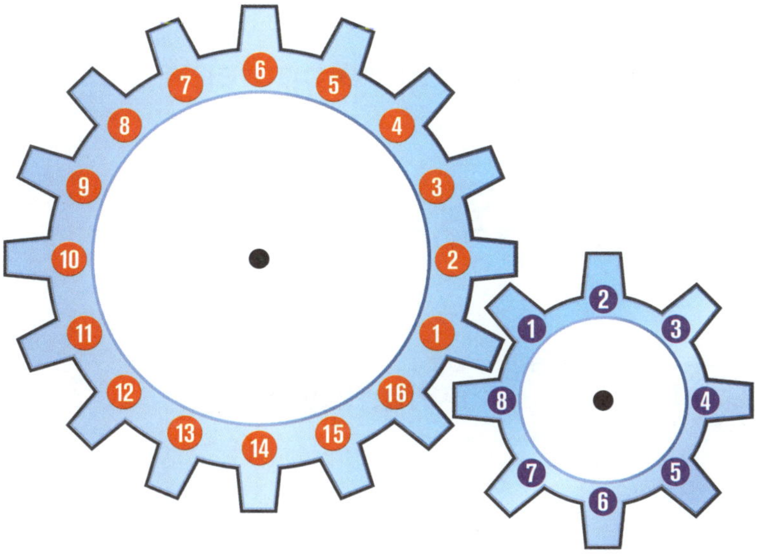

Put together a gear system like you did in the previous exercise, but this time use the 16-tooth gear and one 8-tooth gear. Set them up as shown.

1. If we turn the large gear around once, the small gear turns around 1 / 2 / 3 time(s).

2. The small gear moves faster / slower than the large gear.

3. If we turn the small gear around twice, the large gear goes around 1 / 2 / 3 time(s).

4. The large gear moves faster / slower than the small gear.

5. A gear system can / cannot change the speed of rotation.

Science Corner

When many gears are put together, a gear train is made.

ISBN: 978-1-927042-86-1

7

Try this!

Gears Around Us

- ◯ a disk drive in your computer
- ◯ an electric screwdriver
- ◯ a window blind
- ◯ a wind-up toy
- ◯ an umbrella
- ◯ a tool box
- ◯ a window
- ◯ a printer

Checklist

Are you able to...

- ☐ identify objects that have gears in their mechanisms?
- ☐ make gears to recognize the direction of movements of the gears?
- ☐ make gears to recognize the speeds of the gears?

ISBN: 978-1-927042-86-1

Pulleys

8

In this unit, students will:

- identify different kinds of simple machines.
- identify different objects that contain pulleys and the work that they do.
- learn the mechanism of a fixed pulley.
- learn the mechanism of a movable pulley.

ISBN: 978-1-927042-86-1

8

A. Look at each picture and the words. Name the simple machine that is in use.

lever screw inclined plane
pulley gears wheel and axle

1.

____

2.

____

3.

____

4.

____

5.

____

6.

____

ISBN: 978-1-927042-86-1

B. **Name the object that uses the pulley and describe the work that it does.**

Science Corner

Pulleys are used to move things from one place to another. They make it easier to get work done. We see them being used in many places.

1. 

Object: ____________________

The work that it does:

____

____

2. 

Object: ____________________

The work that it does:

____

____

3. 

Object: ____________________

The work that it does:

____

____

ISBN: 978-1-927042-86-1

8

C. Look at the diagrams. Complete the paragraphs about pulleys with the given words.

Lifting Alone

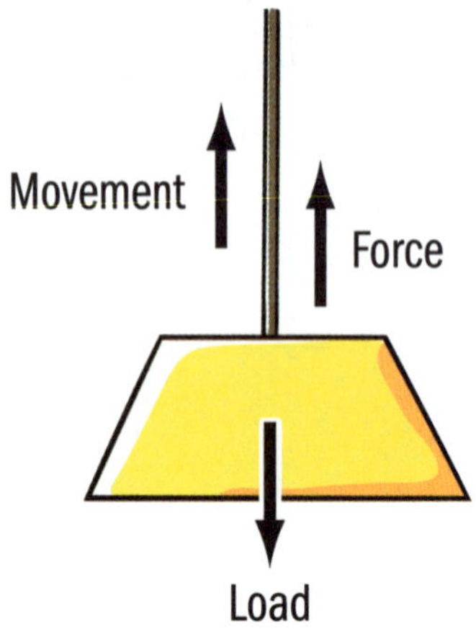

Lifting with a Fixed Pulley

effort fixed force one down
direction muscles weight

If we want to move something, we need to apply a 1. ____________ . We can use a 2. ____________ pulley system to do this. In a system like this, the pulley stays in 3. ____________ place. This system changes the 4. ____________ of the force needed to move something, not the amount of force.

When we pull upward to move something, we are pulling with our 5. ____________ alone. It is usually easier to pull something 6. ____________ rather than pull it up because we can use our 7. ____________ as an additional force. Our muscles lift the load with less 8. ____________ .

ISBN: 978-1-927042-86-1

D. **Read the paragraphs. Label the diagram with the words in bold. Then answer the questions.**

If the pulley is allowed to move, then lifting a load becomes easier. The force needed to move the load is called the ***load force****.*

A ***movable pulley*** *supports and moves with the load. The pulley is attached to the load, and the rope is attached to the* ***ceiling****. This makes lifting the load easier because the rope attached to the ceiling takes half the weight of the load. You only have to use half the* ***effort force*** *that you would use with a fixed pulley system. For example, to lift a 100-kg load, you would only have to use an effort force of 50 kg.*

1. **Lifting with a Movable Pulley**

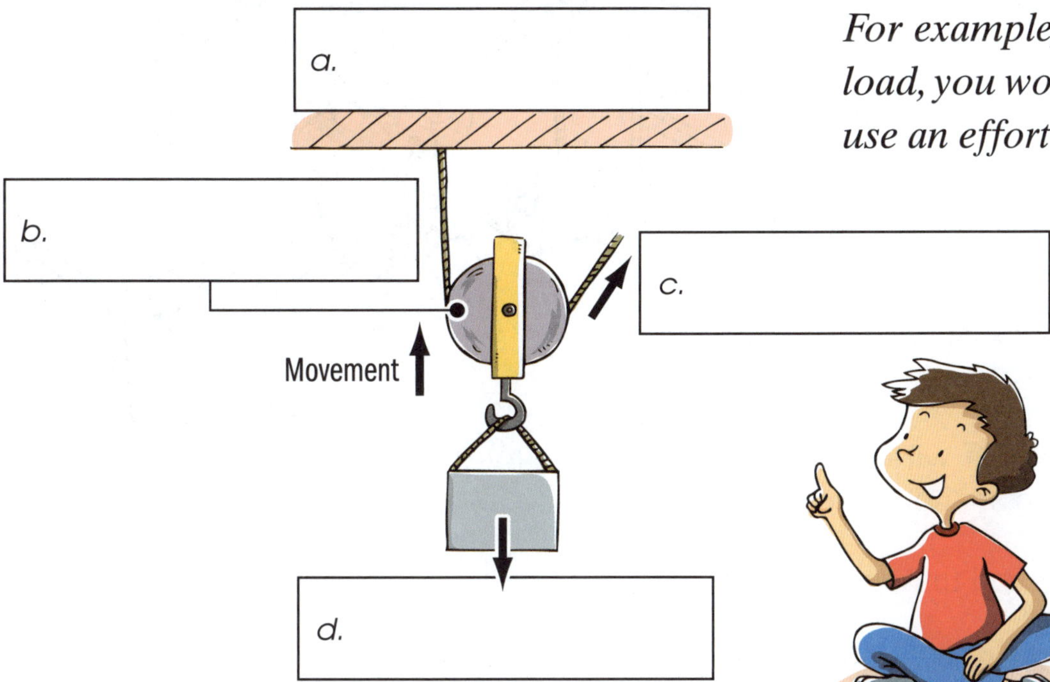

2. What is load force?

___

3. How much effort force would you use to lift a 300-kg weight with a movable pulley system?

___

4. Where does the other effort force come from?

___

8

Try this!

A Good Helper

Materials:

- a stiff wire
- a spool
- a hardcover book
- a rod
- a string

Steps:

1. Thread the stiff wire through the spool and twist the wire to form a loop as shown in the circle.
2. Thread the rod through the loop.
3. Tie the book with the string and place the string over the spool.
4. Use the spool and string as a fixed pulley to lift the book.

Checklist

Are you able to...

- [ ] identify different kinds of simple machines?
- [ ] identify different objects that contain pulleys and the work that they do?
- [ ] tell the mechanism of a fixed pulley?
- [ ] describe the mechanism of a movable pulley?

ISBN: 978-1-927042-86-1

Minerals

9

In this unit, students will:

- find out about mineral facts and identify minerals and rocks.
- fill in the Mohs Scale with the given information.
- describe different minerals by their colour, lustre, and transparency.
- identify minerals by their hardness.

ISBN: 978-1-927042-86-1

9

A. Fill in the blanks with the given words to complete the paragraph.

Mineral Facts

colour hardness minerals crystal
rock shape inorganic

1. ______________ are solid materials that form naturally. They are 2. ______________, which means they are not, and never were, alive. In fact, they are the materials that make up a 3. ______________. A rock may be made up of one or many minerals. Minerals can be different in their 4. ______________, 5. ______________, and 6. ______________, but they are all capable of forming a 7. ______________. The known minerals number in the thousands, yet only a handful make up most of the Earth's solid crust.

B. Look at these samples. Tell whether each of these is a rock or a mineral.

1. ______________ 2. ______________

Science Corner

A mineral is made up of one substance; it is the same inside and out. A rock may be made up of one or more minerals.

ISBN: 978-1-927042-86-1

C. **Read what Mr. Winter says. Help him complete the Mohs Scale with the following information about the minerals.**

The Mohs Hardness Scale lists certain minerals from 1 to 10, with 1 being the softest and 10 being the hardest. A mineral has the ability to scratch another mineral that is softer, but not one that is harder. Every mineral has then been given a hardness number based on its ability to scratch and be scratched.

- **Talc** is the softest mineral.
- **Corundum** is the second hardest.
- **Calcite** is harder that talc and **gypsum** only.
- **Diamond** is harder than corundum.
- **Orthoclase** can scratch **apatite**, but not **quartz**.
- There are four minerals on the scale that apatite can scratch.
- **Fluorite** is harder than calcite and softer than apatite.
- Quartz can be scratched by **topaz**.

Mohs Scale of Hardness

SOFTEST

1	______________
2	______________
3	______________
4	______________
5	______________
6	______________
7	______________
8	______________
9	______________
10	______________

HARDEST

ISBN: 978-1-927042-86-1

9

D. **Use the given descriptive words to describe the minerals.**

Colour	Lustre	Transparency
• yellow	• metallic	• transparent
• green	• dull	• opaque
• colourless	• glassy	

1

Colour: ____________________

Lustre: ____________________

Transparency: ______________

2

Colour: ____________________

Lustre: ____________________

Transparency: ______________

3

Colour: ____________________

Lustre: ____________________

Transparency: ______________

4

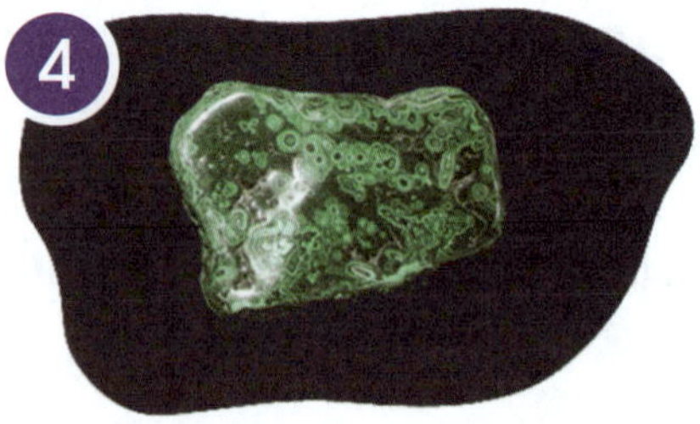

Colour: ____________________

Lustre: ____________________

Transparency: ______________

ISBN: 978-1-927042-86-1

E. Look at the hardness of each mineral described on page 59. Identify each mineral with the help of the following information.

- Pyrite is yellow.
- Halite is transparent.
- Gold is opaque.
- Pyrite can scratch the other three minerals.
- Malachite is harder than calcite.

Mohs Scale of Hardness

1 *Talc*

2 *Gypsum*

3 *Calcite*

4 *Fluorite*

5 *Apatite*

6 *Orthoclase*

7 *Quartz*

8 *Topaz*

9 *Corundum*

10 *Diamond*

1. ______

2. ______

3. ______

4. ______

ISBN: 978-1-927042-86-1

9

Try this!

My Own Crystals

Materials:

- a pencil
- salt
- a string
- water
- a glass

Steps:

1. Add 3 tablespoons of salt to a glass half filled with warm water.
2. Tie a string to a pencil and lay it across the glass so the string dips into the water a bit.
3. Within a few days, salt crystals will form on the string.

Checklist

Are you able to...

- ☐ describe mineral facts and identify minerals and rocks?
- ☐ fill in the Mohs Scale with the given information?
- ☐ describe different minerals by their colour, lustre, and transparency?
- ☐ identify minerals by their hardness?

ISBN: 978-1-927042-86-1

Rocks

10

In this unit, students will:

- learn about different rocks in our environment and the common minerals found in rocks.
- name rocks in different sizes.
- recognize that there are three kinds of rocks.
- learn what quarrying is and the effects of quarrying on our environment.

ISBN: 978-1-927042-86-1

10

A. Read the paragraphs. Then answer the questions.

Rocks are the sand and pebbles on the beach, the mountains we climb, and the ground beneath us. But what are they made up of?

Rocks are all made up of one or more minerals. Different rocks have different combinations and amount of minerals. Some minerals that can be found in rocks are mica, quartz, calcite, and orthoclase.

1. List four examples of rocks around us.

_______________ _______________

_______________ _______________

2. What are rocks made up of?

____

3. Write the mineral content of these rocks.

arkose	granite	marble
• o__________	• o__________	• c__________
• q__________	• q__________	
	• m__________	

ISBN: 978-1-927042-86-1

B. Put the rocks on the scale in order from smallest to largest.

Sizes of Rock

smallest

____

____

____

____

____

____

largest ______________

C. Look at the descriptions. Then identify the rocks.

Kinds of Rocks

- **Igneous** – These rocks form when molten rock from deep in the Earth cools.
- **Sedimentary** – These rocks form when bits of mud, clay, or sand form layers and harden over time.
- **Metamorphic** – This kind of rock forms when one of the other kinds of rocks is under intense heat or pressure.

1. ______________

Examples

- **sandstone:** compressed sand
- **shale:** formed from mud

2. ______________

Examples

- **granite:** cooled slowly underground
- **basalt:** cooled quickly above the surface of the Earth

3. ______________

Examples

- **gnesis:** was once granite
- **marble:** was made from limestone

ISBN: 978-1-927042-86-1

10

D. Guess what the children are talking about. Write the answers on the lines.

fossil igneous metamorphic
minerals rock sedimentary

1.

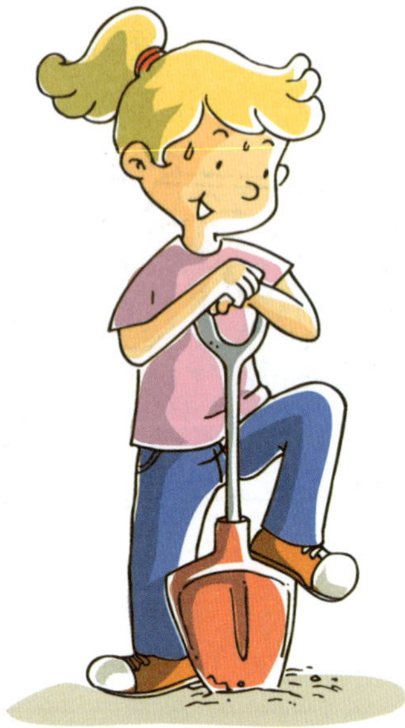

Rock formed from layers of sand, mud, or clay over time

____

Rocks contain at least one of these.

____

2.

The remains of an ancient plant or animal

____

Rock formed from molten rock inside the Earth

____

3.

It is made from one or more minerals.

____

Rock formed from being heated or compressed intensely

____

ISBN: 978-1-927042-86-1

E. **Fill in the blanks with the given words to complete the paragraphs about quarrying. Then answer the questions.**

erosion	mining	plants
quarrying	sediments	trees

We do our share of landscape changing. Removing rocks from the land is called 1. ______________ and removing minerals is called 2. ______________ . While both are necessary to produce the rock materials we need, they can have a big impact on the surrounding environment.

Apparently, quarrying produces 3. ______________ and quickens 4. ______________ . Quarries can limit these effects by keeping 5. ______________ and 6. ______________ in place whenever possible.

7. What impact do you think the quarry has on the environment?

____

____

____

____

____

____

ISBN: 978-1-927042-86-1

10

Try this!

A Rock Expert

Ask your parents to take you to a garden store to take a close look at the rocks sold there. Make a table to record your observations. Then share your knowledge of rocks with your friends. They'll think that you are really a rock expert!

Name	Colour	Texture

Draw pictures of the rocks to go with the descriptions if you like.

Checklist

Are you able to...

- ☐ distinguish different rocks in our environment and the common minerals found in rocks?
- ☐ name rocks in different sizes?
- ☐ tell the three kinds of rocks?
- ☐ explain what quarrying is and the effects of quarrying on our environment?

ISBN: 978-1-927042-86-1

A. **Complete the crossword puzzle.**

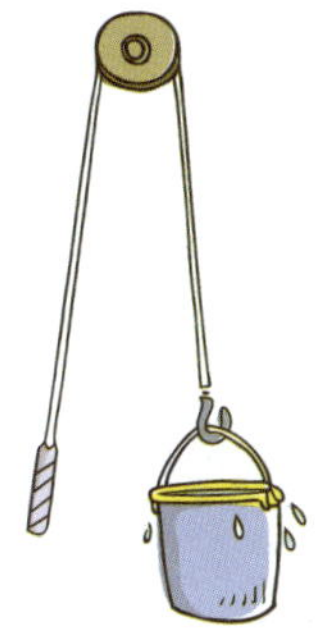

These rocks form when bits of mud, clay, or sand form layers and harden over time.

a rock that was under intense heat or pressure

A rock may be made up of many of these.

The larger this is, the louder the sound.

the remains of an ancient plant or animal

fossil vibration metamorphic

minerals pulley quarrying sedimentary

ISBN: 978-1-927042-86-1

B. Check the correct answers.

1. Alarming sounds:

(A)

(B)

(C)

(D)

(E)

(F)

2. Machines that contain gears:

(A)

(B)

(C)

3. Kinds of rocks:

(A) clay (B) diamond (C) boulder

(D) gold (E) stone (F) mountain

 ISBN: 978-1-927042-86-1

4. Describe the mineral:

Colour	Lustre	Transparency
(A) colourless	(A) dull	(A) opaque
(B) yellow	(B) glassy	(B) transparent

5. A correct sentence that describes the big gear:

(A) The big gear will turn clockwise at a speed that is faster than the small one.

(B) The big gear will turn counterclockwise at a speed that is slower than the small one.

(C) The big gear will turn clockwise at a speed that is the same as the small one.

(D) The big gear will turn counterclockwise at a speed that is faster than the small one.

6. This instrument makes sound with its strings' vibration:

(A) violin
(B) drum
(C) flute
(D) triangle

ISBN: 978-1-927042-86-1

C. Fill in the blanks with the given words.

metamorphic sedimentary igneous

1. Melted rock deep in the Earth comes up through the crust, sometimes as molten lava through a volcano. It cools and hardens.

This is ______________ rock.

2. Wind, rain, and gravity broke down pieces of bigger rock and sand. They collected and settled, layer upon layer. Millions of years later, a kind of rock was formed.

They are ______________ rocks.

3. The Earth changes and some rocks get buried. Heat or pressure changes them, without melting them.

They are ______________ rocks.

Examples of each kind of rock

4. ______________

- **granite:** cooled slowly underground
- **basalt:** cooled quickly above the surface of the Earth

5. ______________

- **sandstone:** compressed sand
- **shale:** formed from mud

6. ______________

- **gnesis:** was once granite
- **marble:** was made from limestone

ISBN: 978-1-927042-86-1

D. Look at the Mohs Scale. Fill in the blanks.

Mohs Scale of Hardness

SOFTEST

1. Talc
2. Gypsum
3. Calcite
4. Fluorite
5. Apatite
6. Orthoclase
7. Quartz
8. Topaz
9. Corundum
10. Diamond

HARDEST

1. Seven minerals in the chart are softer than ______________ .

2. The softest mineral is ______________ .

3. Corundum is softer than ______________ .

4. Fluorite is ______________ than calcite.

5. Quartz is ______________ than topaz.

6. Gypsum is harder than ______________ .

7. ______________ will scratch gypsum but not fluorite.

8. ______________ will scratch apatite but not quartz.

9. Halite can scratch gypsum but not calcite. The scale of hardness of halite is in between ______________ and ______________ .

10. On this scale, each mineral can scratch the ones ______________ (below/above) it, but none can scratch a mineral ______________ (below/above) it.

E. **Look at the scale showing the loudness of a ringing bell. Colour the bar to show the loudness of the noise from each of the things.**

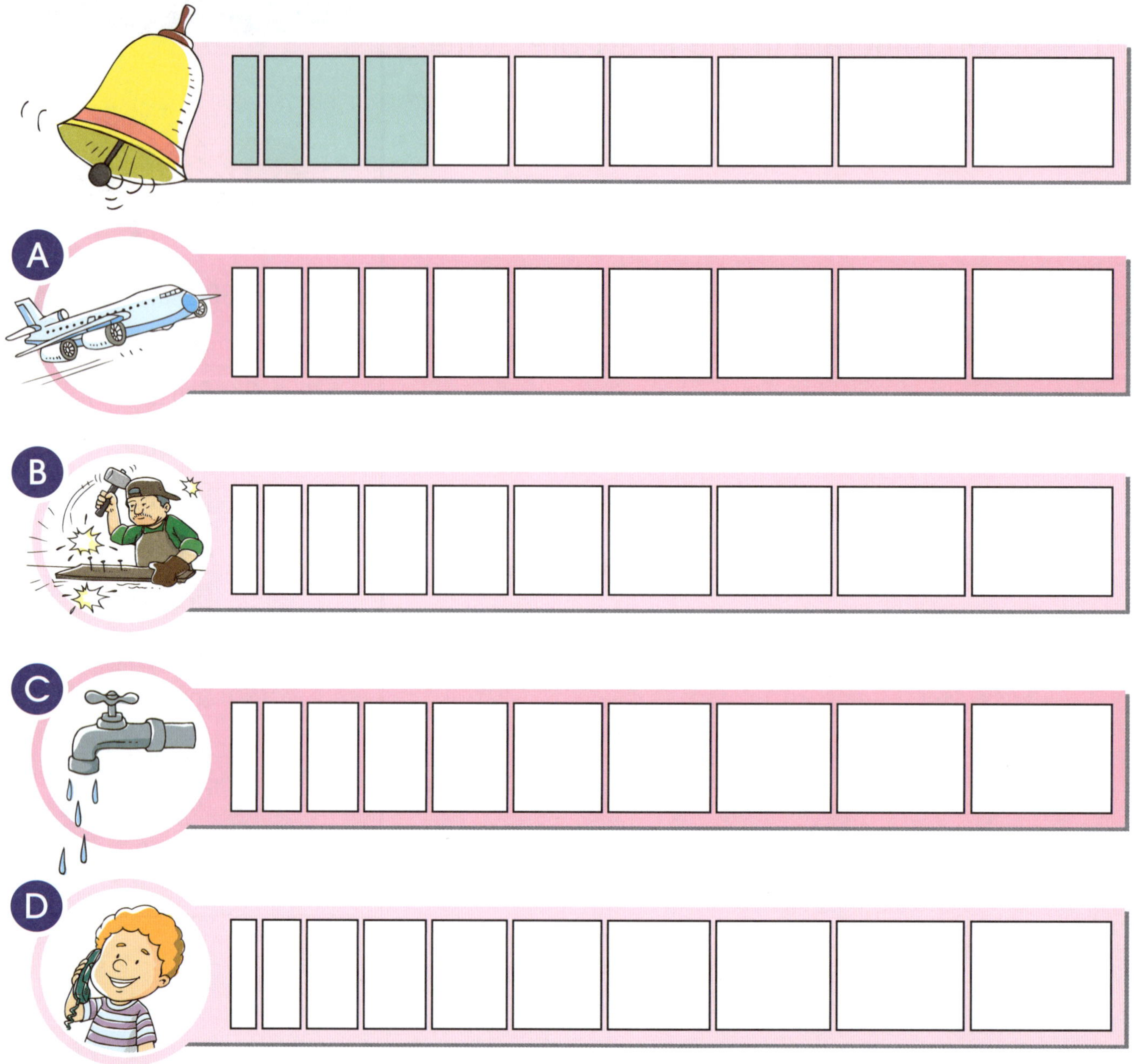

F. **Look at the pictures in the circles above. Match them with the correct readings. Write the letters.**

1. 40 dB ◯

2. 130 dB ◯

3. 20 dB ◯

4. 70 dB ◯

ISBN: 978-1-927042-86-1

Answers

ISBN: 978-1-927042-86-1

ANSWERS

1 Habitats and Communities (1)

A. 1.

	Food	Habitat	Shelter
Wood Duck	water plants and tiny water animals acorns, seeds, and berries	marsh	natural hole in a tree
Beaver	cambium	stream	dam and lodge
White Shark	seals and sea lions	open ocean / shallow water for feeding	

2. ocean
3. (Individual answer)

B. (Individual answer for the additional animal in each column)
1. duck, fish, tadpole, mosquito, goose, turtle
2. mole, worm, groundhog, ant, mite, millipede
3. caterpillar, robin, beetle, owl, monkey, koala

C. 1. bald eagle
2. sow bug
3. marmot
4. beaver

D. 1. C
2. B
3. A

Try this!
(Individual answer)

2 Habitats and Communities (2)

A. 1. sun ; producers
2. consumers
3. community
4. producers
5. sun

B. Producer: pine trees ; birch trees ; mushrooms ; dwarf plants ; grass
Consumer: white-tailed deer ; snowshoe hare ; bobcat ; mountain lion ; polar bear ; arctic fox ; caribou ; lemming

C. 1. Carnivore: animals that eat only flesh ; lion
Herbivore: animals that eat only plants ; rabbit
Omnivore: animals that eat flesh and plants ; chicken
2. omnivore

D. 1. medicine
2. clothing
3. travel
4. shelter
5. food
6. travel
7. A. medicine
B. clothing

Try this!
(Individual observation)

3 Food Chains

A. 1. energy
2. producers
3. Consumers
4. food chains
5.

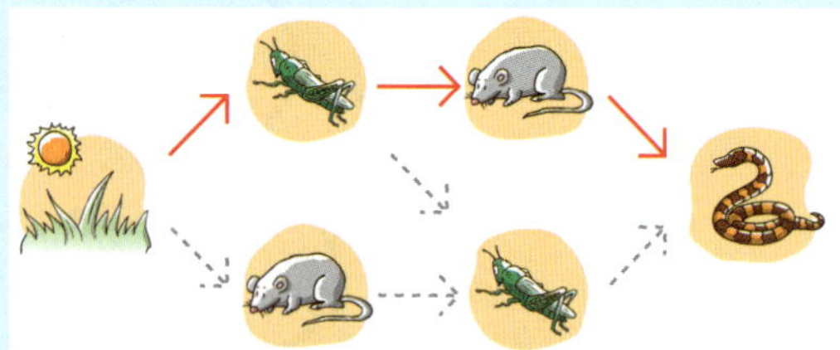

6.

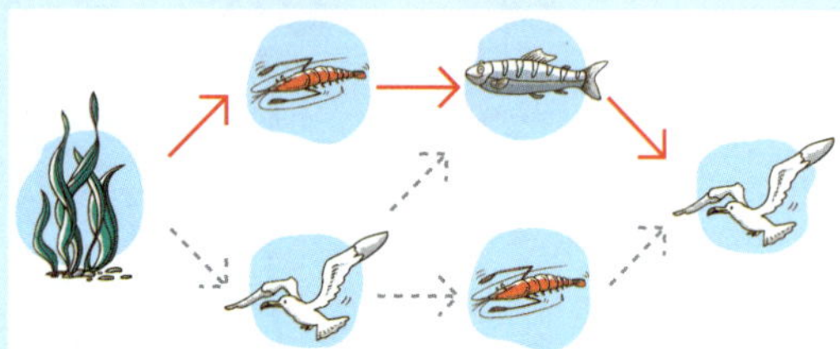

B. A. plant ; mouse ; owl
B. grass → rabbit → red fox → tiger
C. plankton → shrimp → small fish → big fish → shark
D. sage brush → insect → lizard → snake → hawk

C. 1. food chains
2. Healthy
3. disappear
4. break
5. grass → zebra → lion
producer herbivore carnivore

D. Situation 1
a. The amount of grass would increase.
b. The number of lions would decrease.
Situation 2
a. The number of zebras would decrease.
b. The number of lions would decrease.
Situation 3
a. The number of zebras would increase.
b. The amount of grass would decrease.
It is important because we rely much upon them.

ISBN: 978-1-927042-86-1

Try this!

Activity

4 Adaptations of Living Things

A. 1. B
2. C
3. D
4. E
5. A

B. 1. D
2. B
3. A
4. E
5. C

C. 1. butterfly
2. bee
3. fly
4. ant
5. mountain pine beetle
6. mosquito

D. 1. B 2. B
3. B 4. A

Try this!

(Individual answer)

5 Light

A. 1. natural
2. artificial

B.

Natural Light	Artificial Light
lightning stars	fluorescent light lamp streetlight monitor

C. 1. emit
2. reflect
3.

4.

5.

D. 1. natural light ; produces no heat
2. artificial light ; gives off heat
3. natural light ; gives off heat

E. 1. white
2. rainbow
3. spectrum

F. 1. reflection

2. refraction

G. 1. refraction
2. reflection

Try this!

(Individual observation)

ISBN: 978-1-927042-86-1

ANSWERS

Midway Review

A.

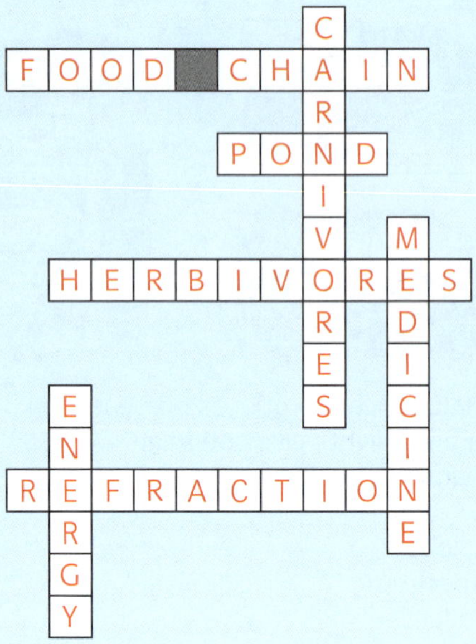

B.
1. B ; D ; E
2. A ; B ; C
3. A ; B
4. C
5. B
6. B
7. B ; D

C.
1. in straight lines from the light source
2. refraction
3. is an example of a light source
4. refracts, displaying the seven colours of the visible spectrum
5. water drops in the air bend sunlight

6 Sound

A. (Individual answers)

B.
1. 10 dB
2. 80 dB
3. 25 dB
4. 100 dB
5. 180 dB
6. 120 dB

C.
1. being struck ; A ; E
2. having air blown into it ; B ; D
3. having strings that vibrate ; C ; F

D.
1. alarming sound
2. detecting sound
3. detecting sound
4. alarming sound
5. soothing sound
6. alarming sound

E. (Suggested answers)
alarming sound: phone ringtone
detecting sound: computer sound from keyboard strokes
soothing sound: piano

Try this!
Activity

7 Gears

A.
1. ✗
2. ✔
3. ✔
4. ✗
5. ✔
6. ✔
7. ✔
8. ✔

C.
1. The other gears turn.
2.

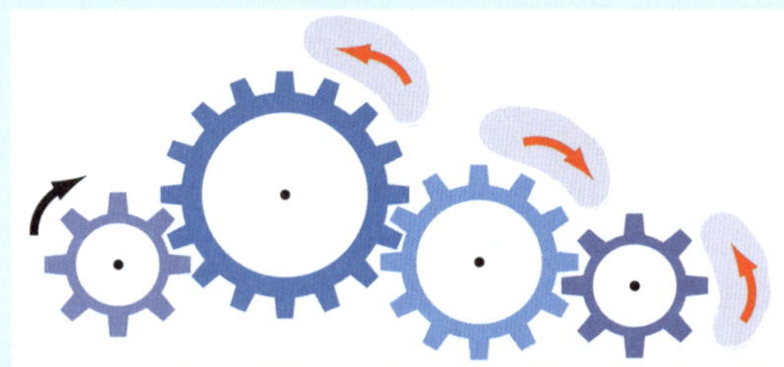

3. clockwise
4. yes

D.
1. 2
2. faster
3. 1
4. slower
5. can

Try this!
(Individual observation)

8 Pulleys

A.
1. pulley
2. screw
3. gears
4. lever
5. inclined plane
6. wheel and axle

B.
1. crane ; lifts heavy loads
2. clothesline ; allows clothes to be hung for drying
3. flagpole ; pulls up a flag

C.
1. force
2. fixed
3. one
4. direction
5. muscles
6. down
7. weight
8. effort

ISBN: 978-1-927042-86-1

D. 1a. ceiling
   b. movable pulley
   c. effort force
   d. load force
   2. It is the force needed to move the load.
   3. I would need an effort force of 150 kg.
   4. The other effort force comes from the ceiling.

Try this!
Activity

9 Minerals

A. 1. Minerals
   2. inorganic
   3. rock
   4-6. colour/hardness/shape
   7. crystal

B. 1. a mineral
   2. a rock

C. 1. Talc
   2. Gypsum
   3. Calcite
   4. Fluorite
   5. Apatite
   6. Orthoclase
   7. Quartz
   8. Topaz
   9. Corundum
   10. Diamond

D. 1. colourless ; glassy ; transparent
   2. yellow ; metallic ; opaque
   3. yellow ; metallic ; opaque
   4. green ; dull ; opaque

E. 1. Halite
   2. Gold
   3. Malachite
   4. Pyrite

Try this!
Activity

10 Rocks

A. 1. sand ; pebbles ; mountains ; ground
   2. Rocks are made up of one or more minerals.
   3. arkose: orthoclase ; quartz
      granite: orthoclase ; quartz ; mica
      marble: calcite

B.

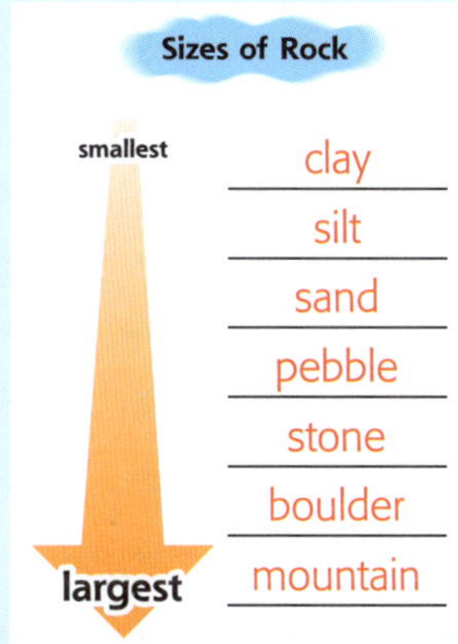

C. 1. Sedimentary
   2. Igneous
   3. Metamorphic

D. 1. sedimentary ; minerals
   2. fossil ; igneous
   3. rock ; metamorphic

E. 1. quarrying
   2. mining
   3. sediments
   4. erosion
   5-6. plants/trees
   7. (Individual answer)

Try this!
(Individual observation)

Final Review

A.

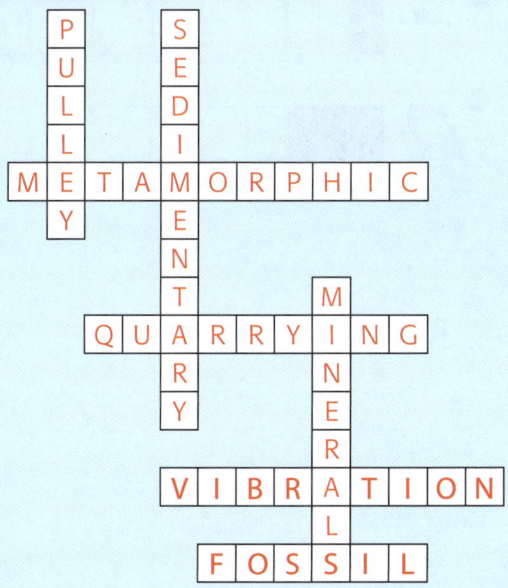

ISBN: 978-1-927042-86-1

ANSWERS

B. 1. B ; C
2. A ; C
3. A ; C ; E ; F
4. Colour: A ; Lustre: B ; Transparency: B
5. B
6. A

C. 1. igneous
2. sedimentary
3. metamorphic
4. igneous
5. sedimentary
6. metamorphic

D. 1. topaz
2. talc
3. diamond
4. harder
5. softer
6. talc
7. Calcite
8. Orthoclase
9. 2 ; 3
10. above ; below

E. (Suggested answers)

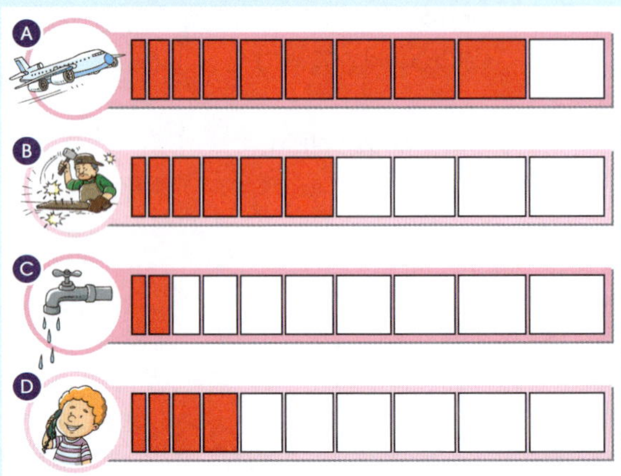

F. 1. D
2. A
3. C
4. B

ISBN: 978-1-927042-86-1